Original title:
Banana Breeze

Copyright © 2025 Creative Arts Management OÜ
All rights reserved.

Author: Eleanor Prescott
ISBN HARDBACK: 978-1-80586-347-2
ISBN PAPERBACK: 978-1-80586-819-4

The Tropic's Soft Caress

In the sun, we dance with glee,
A curious monkey swings from a tree.
With laughter ringing, we share a treat,
Plump and yellow, oh what a feat!

The ocean whispers, salty and sweet,
We gather 'round, adventure at our feet.
With our hats askew and shades so bright,
Chasing coconuts, what a delight!

Whispering Leaves and Laughter

Leaves are rustling, secrets unfold,
Tales of monkeys, cheeky and bold.
Under the shade, we giggle and snack,
As the breeze nudges time, never looks back.

Friends gather close, sharing bright smiles,
The sun radiates joy for miles and miles.
We swing and sway, just being carefree,
In this tropical jungle, come laugh with me!

Golden Moments in the Breeze

Bright yellow treasures in piles on the ground,
We toss them high, laughter all around.
Frolicking under blossoms that sway,
The sweet scent drifts in a playful way.

Chasing shadows as the sun starts to fade,
Imagination sparks, adventures are made.
Silly hats and bright neon shoes,
In this golden glow, we cannot lose!

The Hum of a Summer's Day

Oh, how the sunlight makes us grin,
Frogs are jumping; let the games begin!
With lemonade sips and jokes that soar,
Each moment chuckles, who could ask for more?

Buzzing bees with a little flair,
In our paradise, joy fills the air.
With a hop and a skip, we're feeling grand,
In the warmth of the tropics, hand in hand!

Aromas of Happy Times

In a bowl of smiles, they reside,
Bright yellow jackets, a funny ride.
Slip on their peels, watch folks fall,
Laughter erupts, echoing through the hall.

Swaying in sunlight, they sway and dance,
Whispers of sweetness, a quirky chance.
With every munch, there's a giggle shared,
A fruit-filled party, everyone's cared.

Essence of a Joyful Heart

A pod of giggles in every bite,
Gold nuggets shining, pure delight.
Clever recipes, a treat or two,
Cakes, shakes, and charms, all for you.

Mischief afoot as snacks are served,
Fruity jokes, all perfectly curbed.
A slip here, a laugh there, pure fun,
Sticky fingers when the feast is done.

Warm Winds and Golden Fruit

Breezes blow soft, laughter appears,
Cheeky monkeys bring light-hearted cheers.
Tropical flavors, oh what a thrill,
Each sunny bite, a giggle to fill.

Picnic blankets and chatter galore,
With stories as ripe as fruit we adore.
Sipping smoothies, sharing a grin,
Joy multiplies where good times begin.

Cascades of Tropical Joy

Splashing in sunshine, a fruity delight,
Waves of sweetness, laughter takes flight.
Funny faces on fruit they adore,
Chasing each other, wanting more!

In swirls and twirls, they dance around,
With jiggly giggles, oh what a sound!
Gold on the table, gleaming and bright,
Spreading cheer, a culinary light.

Breezy Adventures on the Edge

Up in the trees, a monkey swings,
With laughter that dances, and silly things.
He steals a snack from a careless chap,
Then races away in a playful clap.

Bright sun above and a breeze below,
Wiggling leaves in a comical show.
A squirrel complains, 'I just lost my lunch!'
But giggles abound in this leafy bunch.

Joyful Whirlwinds of Nature

A whirlwind twirls with a giddy spin,
Chasing the leaves where the fun begins.
Spin, twirl, laugh, and kick up a fuss,
Nature's a playground, no need to rush.

Gentle gusts with a tickle and tease,
Whoops and hollers from buzzing bees.
A butterfly flirts in a dizzy flight,
Winking at folks, what a silly sight!

The Sweetness of An Afternoon

In the soft light of a sunny day,
Fruit falls gently, like laughter at play.
A picnic spread with a colorful taste,
No worries, just giggles, no time to waste.

Jelly jars wobble, and sandwiches grin,
With chips that crinkle as the fun begins.
A parrot squawks, 'Let's dance and cheer!'
While ants hold a parade, drawing quite near.

Glimmers of Cheerful Days

Sunbeams flicker in a quirky dance,
Colors pop out in a joyful prance.
A cat in a hat checks the weather's mood,
He twirls and he laughs; he's the silliest dude.

Laughter echoes from the riverside,
With splashes of fun and a gentle glide.
A frog in the reeds goes ribbit, then croak,
While friends share jokes, in a giggling cloak.

A Heart Full of Warmth

In a land where laughter grows,
Fruits of cheer in sunlit rows.
Peels that slip, oh what a sight,
Chasing joy from morn till night.

The monkeys dance, they swing and sway,
Jokes in fruit, they love to play.
A mango winks, a grape will tease,
As laughter floats upon the breeze.

Whimsical Windfall

A curious fruit fell from the sky,
With giggles wrapped in yellow tie.
It rolled and tumbled, full of cheer,
Making friends with all that's near.

The squirrels laugh, the birds all sing,
A zany twist to every swing.
In every nook, a smile will bloom,
With humor in the orchard's room.

The Glow of Juicy Delight

Round and ripe, they shine so bright,
A citrus burst, pure delight.
With rosy cheeks and silly charms,
They gather close, in joyful swarms.

The juice it splashes, what a scene,
Tickling toes in colors green.
A fruity frolic, laughter flies,
As sweets fall down from sunny skies.

Enchantment in the Orchard

A twisty path through leafy fun,
A place to laugh, to dance, to run.
With whimsy in the air so light,
Every moment feels so right.

Join the parade of giggly friends,
With zesty whispers that never end.
Through orchards bright with joy and glee,
A jolly crowd, so wild and free.

The Fruitful Gaze

In a land where the fruit hangs low,
A monkey peeks with a funny show.
He's swinging high, he's trying to land,
Grabbing a treat with a goofy hand.

The sun shines bright, his belly shakes,
He wobbles around, oh, the laughter wakes!
Each slip and slide, such comic grace,
Join in the giggle, let joy embrace.

Laughter in the Canopy

Treetops sway with a playful tease,
A bird takes flight on a warm, sweet breeze.
It tumbled down, what a sight to see,
Chasing the fruit, oh, wee jubilee!

With every peep, the jungle sings,
Playful critters wearing silly wings.
They tumble and roll in a bright parade,
Under the shade, the fun won't fade.

Breezy Echoes of Paradise

The breeze whistles tunes with a cheeky flair,
A troupe of critters drift without care.
From heights up high, they sway and sway,
Bouncing along, they kick the day.

With a chirp and a laugh, they plot their schemes,
Building a fortress of wacky dreams.
In a world of giggles, they take their stance,
Dancing around as if in a trance.

A Peel of Laughter

With a twist and a turn, the laughter rolls,
A gleeful chase through the leafy knolls.
A slip on the vine, a comical sight,
The giggles erupt, oh what pure delight!

They prance and they play, no worries at all,
As the forest bursts into a laughter call.
Each chuckle echoes through vibrant green,
In this joyful dance, a true comedy scene.

Unfolding Warmth and Whimsy

In the sunbeam's glow, we sway,
With silly smiles, we laugh all day.
A twisty fruit, so bright and bold,
It tickles our hearts, a sight to behold.

The monkeys swing from tree to tree,
Doing flips as if they're free.
A slip and slide on peels of cheer,
Your giggles echo, loud and clear.

Yellow hats and wild balloon fights,
Chasing shadows, our silly sights.
With every bite and the laughter wends,
This joyful dance, it never ends.

So join the fun, don't hesitate,
In this zany world, let's celebrate.
With playful spirits, we won't refrain,
We'll dance again through sunshine and rain.

A Canvas of Golden Mirth

A vibrant hue across the land,
The fruit of laughter in our hand.
Its cheerful shape, a jolly jest,
It brings us joy, we feel so blessed.

With each bright glance, a giggle grows,
A squishy slip, as humor flows.
We toss and juggle with silly flair,
Creating smiles everywhere.

In a hammock swinging, we take a rest,
While jokes fly by, it's simply the best.
Banana hats on goofy heads,
As laughter bounces from the spreads.

One last slide, and we all fall down,
With fruit-filled fun, we wear the crown.
In hearty jest, we find our glee,
A canvas painted, wild and free.

Laughter in the Heart of Nature

In the trees, a monkey swings,
A hat he wears; oh, what a thing!
He turns and laughs, what a scene,
Nature's joy, a vibrant green.

A parrot yells, 'Hey, look at me!'
With colors bright, it's plain to see.
The breeze can tickle, twist, and tease,
While flowers dance in playful ease.

A squirrel sneaks a nut, just right,
Then jumps in fright—a sudden flight!
The world is full of silly tricks,
Nature's jester plays with sticks.

As the sun dips low, the giggles grow,
With every rustle, there's a show.
In this land where trees entwine,
Laughter flows like sweet sunshine.

Echoes of Vibrant Dreams

In fields of gold, the crickets chirp,
With dreams so wild, they dance and burp.
The frogs join in with leaps so grand,
Their chatter spreads across the land.

A turtle crawls with quiet pride,
While butterflies take joyride.
The flowers sway, they can't resist,
In nature's realm, no one is missed.

The breeze brings tales from far away,
Of silly things that love to play.
A juggler's act with fruits in hand,
A carnival in this great land.

As stars peek out, the giggles stay,
In echoes soft, they'll find their way.
With every dream that takes its flight,
There's laughter shared in the moonlight.

A Tasting of Sunlight

In patches bright, the daisies grin,
With yummy thoughts of sugar, skin.
A picnic spread with snacks galore,
Makes nature's laughter hard to ignore.

The ants march in, a tiny parade,
In regimented lines, they invade.
With crumbs of joy, they dance around,
A feast so sweet, laughter is found.

The clouds above have cakes and pies,
While sunbeams twinkle like surprise.
Each ray is a spoon to taste the day,
In golden hues, the giggles play.

As evening comes, the chill arrives,
But in our hearts, the warmth survives.
We share our tales, both wild and bright,
In joyous feasts of pure daylight.

Sunshine's Gentle Embrace

A gentle ray warms silly toes,
As laughter bursts from petals' bows.
The bumblebees dance with delight,
In gardens filled with pure delight.

The breeze tickles the swaying grass,
While squirrels dash, they love to pass.
A dance-off starts, who will win?
With silly moves, let the games begin!

The sun flips pancakes on the lake,
Where fish jump out for joy to shake.
A flick of tail, a splash, a cheer,
This sunny world is full of cheer.

As day drifts low, the shadows play,
In laughter's glow, we'll find our way.
With nature's grin, we'll never part,
For sunshine lives within the heart.

Ribbons of Yellow Laughs

In the orchard, pranks abound,
Laughter echoes all around.
Peels are slipping, slips are made,
Chasing smiles in the sunlit glade.

Silly monkeys swing with flair,
Joking squirrels toss in the air.
Fruit flies dance with silly spins,
As giggles burst from joyful grins.

Hats of fruit upon our heads,
Spinning tales on grassy beds.
A yellow feast, we munch and play,
Giggle fests all through the day.

With every wave of playful jest,
Laughter shines, unlike the rest.
Savoring fun beneath the trees,
In the breeze, our hearts feel free.

Fluttering in the Sunshine

Golden laughter fills the air,
With playful spirits everywhere.
Fluttering hats, in colors bright,
Chasing giggles under the light.

Silly critters in a race,
Rolling quickly, what a chase!
A gentle breeze brings forth a cheer,
As chuckles echo, loud and clear.

The sunbeams play upon my nose,
While laughter blossoms like a rose.
In this garden, joy takes flight,
With every giggle, hearts feel light.

In the warm embrace of day,
We dance and shout; we laugh and sway.
With each silly trick we weave,
In sunshine's glow, we dare believe.

Games of the Garden

In the garden, oh what fun,
Playing games with everyone.
Hide and seek among the vines,
While the sun above brightly shines.

Squirrels giggle, they can't hide,
In windy homes, they safely bide.
Ticklish grass beneath our feet,
Every corner, new friends meet.

Hopscotch laid with petals bright,
Skipping happily, pure delight.
With every laugh, the world feels new,
In the garden, joy broke through.

We toss the fruit, it splats and flies,
Painted faces catch surprise.
In laughter's grip, we burst and play,
In games of joy, we lose our way.

Verdant Revelry

Under leafy canopies, so lush,
We gather round, in playful rush.
Joking roots and dancing leaves,
Create a world where laughter weaves.

Bouncing blooms in a jolly trance,
As tulips sway and daisies dance.
With every cheer, the colors blend,
In this celeb, the fun won't end.

We twirl and twist, a joyous spin,
Crazy hats and goofy grins.
In the verdant shade, we find our glee,
Every chuckle—like confetti free.

Echoing laughter, purest delight,
Under the sun, till the stars ignite.
In the revelry, we share our dreams,
In nature's lap, nothing's as it seems.

Bursting with Nature's Sweetness

In gardens bright with yellow cheer,
A fruit parade, oh what a year!
They slip and slide on sunny days,
Creating laughter, joyous plays.

With every peel, a giggle grows,
They somersault, like tiny pros.
In smoothies whirl, they dance around,
Whipped cream crowned, they're glory-bound.

Swinging from trees in playful jest,
They tease the bees, it's all a fest.
With every bite, a burst of glee,
Nature's jesters, wild and free.

Sunlit Echoes of Playful Days

In warm sunbeams, they take a leap,
Fun yellow blimps, no time for sleep!
A picnic scene with laughter loud,
As fruity friends take center crowd.

They juggle joy in bright arrays,
And hop along the summer rays.
Whispers of giggles fill the air,
With every twist, a quirky flair.

They tuck away in funny hats,
And tease the kittens, dogs, and chats.
Bouncing around with silly prance,
A golden show, a silly dance!

A Palette of Joyful Hues

With splashes bright on canvas wide,
Nature's jesters, what a ride!
Painted smiles in glaring sun,
A wacky world of fruit-filled fun.

In spirals twirl of slippy skins,
Laughter ripples, joy begins.
They dapple fields with vibrant flair,
A carnival, they light the air.

In daisy chains and sandy dunes,
They sport big shades, humming tunes.
Chasing clouds, a joyful spree,
Amidst the giggles, wild and free.

Driftwood and Dreamscapes

Upon the shore, they ride the breeze,
Whimsical fables, driftwood tease.
A fruity band on sandy stage,
Crafting laughs, page after page.

They surf the waves with silly grace,
A fruit-shaped rocket in the race.
Each tumble brings a hearty cheer,
They splash the waves without a fear.

Their timeless tales of fruity fun,
Fill every heart beneath the sun.
With every peel, a story spun,
Dreamscapes linger, laughter won!

Tropical Whispers

In the sun where the fruits all play,
Laughter echoes in a bright bouquet.
Monkeys dance with a silly spin,
Chasing dreams on a fruity whim.

Coconuts drop with a friendly thump,
While silly crabs do the beachy jump.
Parrots squawk in the palm tops high,
Whispering secrets to the sky.

A breeze blows soft with a tropical tease,
Tickling noses with playful ease.
Though the sun may shine with a golden gleam,
There's always room for a giggly dream.

Sunlit Curves

Round and bright like a playful ball,
The trees sway gently, they stand so tall.
Sandy feet in a sunny race,
Jumping high with a goofy face.

Surfers riding waves with grace,
Splashing friends in an oceanic chase.
Drinks with umbrellas, just for fun,
Sipping laughter under the sun.

Tropical fruits, a knobby cheer,
Nonsense jokes fill the atmosphere.
Under the shade, a snooze sounds fine,
Dreaming of joy in lazy line.

The Lullaby of Yellow

Soft yellow hues in the afternoon,
A gentle sway, a teasing tune.
Silly bugs in a bug parade,
Wagging their tails, they're unafraid.

Fluffy clouds in a playful chase,
Dancing softly, a breezy grace.
As the day drifts, giggles bloom,
In the night, the stars find room.

A sleepy breeze sings a mellow roam,
While crickets hum, it feels like home.
With every tickle, a fun surprise,
Under the moon's watchful eyes.

Gentle Auras of the Tropics

In the twilight where the colors mix,
Nature plays its crafty tricks.
Fireflies flicker, a glowing crew,
Whispering tales of the likely dew.

Palm fronds sway in a rhythmic dance,
While iguanas take a daring chance.
Crispy chips from a tropical feast,
With salsa dips that never cease.

Laughter rolls like a sweet serenade,
Under the stars, all worries fade.
With every wave that kisses the shore,
The fun just keeps urging for more.

Ripe with Possibility

In the sun, a fruit doth sway,
A peel so bright, it calls to play.
With laughter bubbling like a brook,
It wears a smile, just take a look.

When mischief dances in the air,
Friends toss ideas without a care.
A creamy dream, delicious cheer,
Each giggle brings more joy, I hear.

And when it slips, oh what a sight,
A slapstick moment, pure delight!
The laughter echoes, light and free,
As we embrace our jubilee.

A Dance Beneath the Tropics

Underneath the palm trees tall,
They sway and twist, we heed the call.
With every step, a vibrant beat,
We shuffle forth on sandy feet.

The fruit is ripe, the spirit high,
We twirl and spin beneath the sky.
With playful jests and silly moves,
This joyous rhythm truly grooves.

A hat askew, a cheeky grin,
A splatter here—a sticky win.
With laughter loud, we find our way,
In dancing shadows, we will stay.

The Joyous Gathering

Gather round, it's time to feast,
A party spread from west to east.
With vibrant laughs, we share a bite,
Each tasty smile ignites the night.

A juggling act of sweet delight,
Silly slips and joyous flight.
With every cheer that fills the room,
We banquet on our shared perfume.

As tales unfold and friends unite,
The atmosphere grows warm and bright.
A mash of voices, songs embrace,
We dance in time, a lively space.

Lush Silhouettes against the Sky

Silhouettes against the light,
Bold and comical in their height.
They sway and twist with playful grace,
Each character finds its place.

A friendly tug, a cheeky poke,
In this bright world, we all invoke.
With silly faces, laughter flows,
In wild shapes, our humor glows.

As shadows flicker, joy ignites,
In this grand dance, we feel delight.
A lively sketch against the sun,
Together here, we're all just one.

Golden Curves of Joy

In the jungle's sunlit halls,
A yellow friend just rolls and falls.
With laughter ringing through the trees,
It dances on the playful breeze.

Rounded shapes, a jolly sight,
They giggle in the morning light.
While monkeys swing, they jabber and squeak,
Our fruity friend, so bright, so chic!

Slipping here and slipping there,
Oh, watch them bounce without a care!
A fruit parade, oh what a scene,
The jester of the jungle green!

In smoothies mixed or cakes so sweet,
Their laughter makes our joy complete.
With every bite, a burst of cheer,
Golden curves, we hold you dear!

Dancing on the Orchard Wind

The orchard sways, the trees all sway,
As fruit begins its hilarious play.
With each gust, they twist and twirl,
It's nature's fun, a fruity whirl!

Joyful echoes fill the air,
A fruit ballet, with flair to spare.
Round and bright, in pairs they sway,
It's a silly, sunny cabaret!

Watch them jiggle, watch them roll,
Against the fence, they'd love to stroll.
With laughter echoing like a tune,
They dance beneath the golden moon!

So grab a friend and join the spree,
In the wind, just let it be.
In silly steps we all abound,
In this orchard, joy is found!

A Serenade to Yellow

Oh merry sphere of sunny hue,
In fruit salads, we adore you!
With peels so bright, a cheerful sight,
A quirky star, a pure delight.

We sing your praises, soft and sweet,
For every snack, you can't be beat!
In every dish, you're sure to steal,
The laughter brings a happy meal!

With silly games like toss and catch,
You raise the stakes, you're quite a match!
In pudding bowls or on a plate,
Your golden glow, we celebrate!

In songs and jokes, you take the lead,
To bring us joy, you are indeed!
So here's to laughter, here's to cheer,
A serenade, we hold you dear!

Sweet Sunshine Dreams

Underneath the sky so blue,
In dreamland, there's a fruit or two.
They giggle softly, take a dive,
In sunny slumber, they arrive!

Floats of laughter, clouds of fun,
Each yellow friend beams in the sun.
In dreamt-up lands, they twist and glide,
On sweetened winds, they laugh and ride.

A hammock swing beneath the trees,
With whispers carried on the breeze.
Oh what a world, so filled with glee,
Sweet sunshine dreams, just you and me!

In each bright vision, joy we glean,
In every flavor, life's a dream.
So raise your cup to laughter's scheme,
Together living sunshine dreams!

Echoes of Sunlit Isles

On shores where laughter sways,
The fruit's in quite a daze.
With peels of yellow cheer,
We dance without a fear.

The waves are chuckling too,
In shorts of vibrant hue.
A seagull steals a bite,
And squawks with pure delight.

Beneath a coconut tree,
We giggle, wild and free.
With smiles that brightly shine,
Our joy is sweet like wine.

Oh, how the sun does glow,
In breezes soft and slow.
With fruity jokes in hand,
We laugh across the land.

A Melody of Sun-Kissed Fruit

In orchards lush and grand,
We frolic in the sand.
With melodies that hum,
We can't help but be dumb.

A monkey swings around,
He's puzzled by the sound.
As laughter fills the air,
We pull our fruit to share.

With splashes in the sea,
We sing so joyfully.
A slip, a slide, a fall,
Our glee will outlast all.

The juiciest of gags,
We wear our fruity rags.
In sunshine's warm embrace,
Happiness finds its place.

Breezy Tranquility

The breeze is blowing light,
Our spirits take to flight.
With giggles in our toes,
We toss the fruit, it glows.

In flip-flops, we will race,
A sunbeam on our face.
We spin and twirl around,
While fruity laughs abound.

A parrot joins the fun,
He squawks, "Let's all run!"
As bubbles fill the air,
Our worries, none can share.

With every sunny glance,
We take a silly chance.
In this tropical state,
We find our festive fate.

Harvest of Sunshine

In fields where giggles grow,
We chase the one who's slow.
With baskets made of dreams,
We gather hearty themes.

Each fruit's a silly sprite,
It winks with pure delight.
We toss them in a pile,
Then gather up our style.

A toss, a fruit-filled game,
And no one feels the shame.
With grins so big they span,
We're just a silly band.

Harvesting joy today,
In our own funny way.
With laughter 'neath the sun,
Our goofy times are fun!

Sunlit Swirls of Happiness

In the sun, we dance and sway,
With goofy grins, we laugh and play.
A fruit that brings a silly cheer,
Brings sunshine even when it's drear.

We juggle rounds with twinkling eyes,
Falling flat, we hear the sighs.
The laughter echoes through the day,
As peels get tossed in wild display.

Harvesting Warmth and Joy

Fields of yellow, bright and bold,
Stories shared, a joy to behold.
We toss a fruit, we catch its flight,
Catching giggles, hearts so light.

A picnic spread beneath the trees,
While breezes play and tease.
With every bite, a messy drape,
Our laughter wraps like a warm escape.

The Art of Sunkissed Whimsy

Sunkissed laughter fills the air,
As we snack without a care.
In a flip, a trip, oh what a sight,
A fruit parade, pure delight!

Dancing peels go flying high,
With every slip, a giggle's nigh.
A playful chase, round and round,
With bright spirits, joy is found.

Nature's Silken Tapestry

We weave a tale with vibrant threads,
Of fruity splendor, laughter spreads.
In woven patterns, we stand tall,
With whimsies large, we'll never fall.

A smooth delight, a joyful quest,
Wrapped in laughter, it's the best.
With every taste, a memory spun,
In our hearts, the joy's just begun.

A Drift of Positively Sunny Moments

In a land where fruit falls free,
Laughter echoes, oh so glee!
Monkeys dance, they sing a tune,
Chasing shadows, morning to noon.

Jokes like peels, they slip and slide,
Witty jests, we cannot hide.
Giggles burst like sunlight beams,
In this place of silly dreams.

Purple skies and yellow sights,
Kites that soar to dizzy heights.
Every step, a spark of cheer,
Joyful moments, far and near.

So come along, let's take a ride,
On a wave of laughter, we glide.
With a twist and a twirl so bright,
Our hearts are light, oh what a sight!

Breezy Rhythms and Golden Smiles

Swaying limbs in gentle breeze,
Tickled toes and funny knees.
Golden rays in playful chase,
Painted smiles on every face.

Dance like leaves in sunny air,
Bumbling bees and buzzing hair.
Frolic, roll, and skip with glee,
Underneath the swaying tree.

Lemonade in striped glass cups,
Bouncing laughter, silly ups.
Juggling fruit, a comic show,
Witty quips, they steal the glow.

So join this jolly, sunny game,
We'll all be laughing just the same.
With every twirl and every spin,
In this humor, we'll always win!

Sunkissed Meanderings

Wandering through a laughing land,
With mischief brewed in every hand.
Flip-flops flop, we jump and shout,
Hooray for fun, there's no doubt!

Bouncing balls and goofy glee,
Sliding down a fruity spree.
A playful breeze will spin us round,
As sunshine twirls on playful ground.

Picnics filled with silly bites,
Tickling toes beneath sunlights.
Each moment blooms like flowers new,
Joy keeps shining, all day through.

So take it easy, feel the play,
Life's a joke in a sunny way.
Let's frolic wildly, lose the strain,
In this laughter, we'll remain!

Radiance in the Shade

Under canopies of laughter's art,
We sip our drinks, a joyful chart.
Each shade a story, bright with light,
In this happy dance, we take flight.

Giggling with our fruity friends,
Witty tales and playful bends.
Life's a circus, let it flow,
With every smile, our joy will grow.

Brightly clad in colors bold,
Silly secrets to be told.
Running wild from sun to shade,
In the fun parade we've made.

So join the cheer, let hearts unite,
In this rhythm of pure delight.
We'll linger here, let laughter reign,
In shadows cast, joy is our gain!

Serenity Amongst the Leaves

On a sunny day, a monkey pranced,
Wearing shades, he took a stance.
Tickling branches, with a grin,
He shook the fruits like a playful win.

A gentle breeze, with laughter calls,
Through the palms, it dances and sprawls.
Coconuts tumble from above,
Pouring rain of tropical love.

Sipping sunshine, the squirrels cheer,
Catching rays, no hint of fear.
In this grove, the giggles glide,
A jungle party, the lazy slide.

Joking lizards in a race,
Winking at their leafy space.
As fireflies bring the night,
Laughter sparkles, pure delight.

The Sweet Dance of Wind.

Whispers of the breeze so sweet,
Fruits enchanting, oh what a treat!
Parrots squawk in comic play,
  Turning ordinary into a ballet.

A gusty laugh ruffles my hair,
As the breeze dances without a care.
Candles flicker, shadows play,
  A fruity twist on a breezy day.

With every twist, the petals sway,
  In a silly twirl, they sashay.
Mangoes rolling with such glee,
Turning the air into pure jubilee.

Sunset paints the sky bright gold,
While the breeze tells stories old.
A carnival of scents perfume,
  In this lovely, juicy room.

Tropical Whispers

The breeze tiptoes, wearing smiles,
Like a clown, it skips for miles.
Whispers of coconuts and cheer,
As the jungle leans in to hear.

A quick-witted iguana basks,
Juggling fruits, oh, what a task!
In a shade that's cool and neat,
Where jokes and laughter meet.

Swaying plants join in the fun,
Making shadows that dance and run.
Clouds burst forth in fits of laughter,
As the day and night chase after.

Giggles swirl in the evening light,
In this land of pure delight.
Where every rustle carries grace,
In this wacky, happy place.

Sun-Kissed Folly

Underneath the golden sun,
A fruit parade, oh what fun!
Maracas hidden in the leaves,
While the wind up the mischief weaves.

A sly raccoon, with brown and white,
Steals a snack, what a sight!
Bouncing berries like a ball,
They tumble down, and one and all.

Dancing shadows spin around,
As laughter echoes, a joyful sound.
The breeze spins tales of silly bliss,
In the land where fun's never amiss.

With sunset hues and playful dreams,
The day ends with silly schemes.
A perfect close in nature's play,
Where the sun and laughter stay.

In the Shade of Palms

Underneath the leafy crowns,
Monkeys swing and dance around.
Coconuts drop with a thud,
Splashing folks in tasty mud.

A picnic spread with fruits so bright,
Bees buzzing in playful flight.
A lizard struts in sandals bold,
Telling tales that never get old.

Sipping drinks of vibrant hue,
Slip and slide, we laugh anew.
The sun's a jester, bright and warm,
In this playful tropical charm.

So let's lounge and take a break,
Join the fun, for goodness' sake!
With every laugh, the world's a stage,
Under palms, we just engage.

Gentle Ribbons of Light

Sunbeams dance on quiet waves,
A playful breeze, the palm tree sways.
Whimsical thoughts float on by,
As kites and laughter fill the sky.

Clouds in shapes of silly things,
One looks like a duck with wings!
Watch the seagulls dive and swoop,
In this sunny, giggly troop.

Uncle Bob forgets his hat,
Children giggle, 'Look at that!'
With goofy grins, the day rolls on,
As the golden rays keep shining strong.

Silly games beneath the sun,
Who knew life could be this fun?
With every chuckle, every cheer,
We find joy in the atmosphere.

Swaying in the Afternoon

Waves of laughter roll through the air,
Swaying gently without a care.
A hammock swings, a nap on cue,
But first, a tickle to wake up you!

Bright parrots squawking silly tunes,
Dancing shadows underneath moons.
High above, a kite takes flight,
Catching giggles with pure delight.

Ice cream drips upon a nose,
Everyone giggles, oh, who knows?
Slips and trips while grabbing snacks,
Belly laughs fill up our packs.

As sunset paints the skies so sweet,
Age-old tales resound and meet.
In this magic afternoon,
Life's a party, like a cartoon!

Nature's Creamy Delight

Smooth and sweet, the fun unfolds,
Ice cream cones in colors bold.
A picnic spread with splashes bright,
In nature's arms, we feel just right.

A squirrel steals a juicy treat,
While giggling kids jump to their feet.
Tickling senses with every bite,
In this sunny, joyous light.

Painting faces, wild and weird,
As laughter bubbles, none are feared.
A dance-off here beneath the trees,
As branches sway like playful seas.

Yellow drips from an ice-cream cone,
With every munch, we claim our throne.
In nature's twist, we find our flight,
Creating laughter, pure delight!

Gentle Breezes of Thoughtful Delights

In a land where monkeys swing,
The laughter of the trees can sing.
Leaves dance gently in the air,
As smiles spread everywhere.

A fruit parade upon the ground,
With silly hats, they spin around.
Whispers of joy float on the breeze,
Tickling toes of clumsy peas.

The sunbeams play peek-a-boo,
While giggles echo clear and true.
Each swing and sway, a comedy show,
With nature's jesters, all aglow.

In this realm of giggles bright,
Every fruit has pure delight.
A world where humor finds its place,
And even the shadows wear a face.

Soft Emotions in the Warmth

Under soft rays of buttery gold,
The warmth makes even the shy ones bold.
Joy bubbles up like fizzy drink,
As critters gather, make us think.

The breeze delivers a fluffy tale,
Of silly squirrels and their grand sail.
With acorns piled like a feast,
They dance around like a lively beast.

Every gust brings a chuckle near,
A symphony of giggles clear.
Soft whispers tickle cheek and ear,
In nature's playground, there's no fear.

With each twist and turn we find,
Relaxed and playful, hearts entwined.
The sheer delight of sunny days,
Dances softly in sunlit rays.

The Silken Touch of Nature's Bliss

Silk-like clouds pass lazily by,
As critters flit and butterflies fly.
A tickle here, a sprightly dance,
Inviting all to take a chance.

With colors bright and spirits high,
A rainbow smiles across the sky.
Sweet aromas make noses twitch,
As laughter joins the playful pitch.

Tick-tock, time sways on a vine,
With every giggle, we feel divine.
The earth beneath, a stage for cheer,
Where even the grumps have to steer.

Join the fun, don't be shy,
Let your silly side fly high.
In this canvas of warmth and glee,
There's room for all in harmony.

Fluttering Dreams in the Grove

In the grove where laughter plays,
All worries drift like wiggly rays.
Wiggly worms write silly rhymes,
As crickets chirp in funny chimes.

The breezy whispers share a joke,
With every rustle, the leaves provoke.
Silly shadows dance on the grass,
Making moments fly by fast.

Fruit lovers gather with delight,
Underneath the starry night.
With lighthearted hearts and playful charms,
Nature's hugs will keep us warm.

In this whimsical, lively space,
Every creature wears a grin on its face.
With giggles echoing through the wood,
It's a world where joy is understood.

Luscious Serenade

A monkey danced on a bright yellow chair,
He juggled fruit with utmost care.
A giggle sprang from the silly feast,
As he shared his snack with a hungry beast.

In the sun, all colors start to swirl,
With laughter and joy, they twist and twirl.
Chasing shadows and clouds above,
A fruity party, oh what a love!

With each bite, a burst of delight,
The world seems fresher, oh so bright.
Slipping and sliding in fruity fun,
Who knew snacks could weigh a ton?

At dusk, they sang a sweet refrain,
Of overloaded laughter and a tiny pain.
With cans of juice like a river flow,
All under a sunset's golden glow.

The Goblet of Warmth

A goblet splashed with sunny cheer,
Holding secrets that tickle your ear.
Sipped with giggles, it's fruity hay,
Each gulp a twisty, funny ballet.

Straws like snakes in a bubbling pool,
Riding waves, oh what a fool!
With tiny umbrellas in a sunny scene,
They dance and sway, oh how they preen!

Laughter froth over the colorful rim,
Take a sip and do a whim!
With every pour, a joke will rise,
From the fish that swims with googly eyes.

As night descends, their stories thrill,
With fruit-infused laughs that surely chill.
Cheeky cups keep the spirits high,
In this goblet, we all can fly.

Vertical Dreams of the Tropics

Up in the trees, where the monkeys swing,
They plot and plan for the fruity fling.
With giggles echoing through green vines,
Imagining what in midst of sunshine shines.

A parrot squawks with a cheeky grin,
His feathers bright, a flashy win.
Jumping from branch to branch, oh so spry,
He claims he's the king with a jolly high!

Bouncing and rolling down from the sky,
With every tumble, just let out a sigh.
In dreams of delight, they surf on the breeze,
Finding treasures tucked behind giggling leaves.

When the sun dips low, the stars arise,
Jokes of the day fill the tropical skies.
With chuckles and hiccups, they rest their heads,
In vertical dreams, where laughter spreads.

Unfolding Petals of Joy

In a garden of glee, petals dance,
With every gust, they take a chance.
Bright colors tumble, a joyful spree,
As critters giggle beneath the tree.

Each leaf whispers tales of sweet delight,
Of sneaky bugs that dance at night.
Fluttering smiles in the balmy air,
Tickled by breezes, without a care.

Bouncing blooms in a merriment swirl,
Round and round in a dizzy twirl.
Petals unfurling with curious charm,
Wrap us softly in nature's arm.

With laughter echoing, they play all day,
In fields of color, they laugh and sway.
Unfolding joy in every sunny patch,
With petals of laughter, none can scratch!

Whispering Palms

In the shade where tall trees sway,
Chatter of leaves welcomes the day.
Squirrels dance with nimble feet,
Unexpected guests, oh what a treat!

Fronds tickle the air like a joke,
Laughter erupts from a teasing poke.
The breeze giggles like a playful child,
Whispers of folly running wild!

Lemons drop in a comedic crash,
While coconuts join in with a splash.
Sunshine beams like a funny face,
Nature's circus, a wild embrace!

So let's sway with the leaves on high,
Watching the world as it zooms by.
In this dance of the frolic and tease,
We find our joy in the whispering breeze.

Nature's Silken Caress

Oh, the tickle of grass invites a laugh,
Unruly kids take the silliest path.
Butterflies flutter in a roundabout,
While raindrops play tag: 'You're it!' - shout!

Petals giggle as they take to the floor,
The rhythm of nature, a dance to explore.
An ant dons a hat and struts with flair,
A common critter, but debonair!

Clouds drift by in their lazy attire,
While sunlight zips in a cheerful choir.
Each breeze carries secrets of old,
Funny tales that even rocks have told!

With whispers of silk, the world comes alive,
In the laughter of leaves, we joyfully thrive.
Here's to the quirks that nature bestows,
In this vibrant chaos, our spirit grows!

Cascade of Tropic Delights

Waterfalls tumble with a splashy cheer,
While curious frogs croak songs that we hear.
Every plop and every crack,
Turns the mundane into a laughing act!

Mangoes roll down like playful bombs,
Hopping around, oh what fun comms!
Pineapples giggle in fruity delight,
Each twist and turn is a comical sight.

A parrot mimics an old silly tune,
Underneath the watchful sun and moon.
Laughter reverberates through the trees,
Nature's joke shop, oh how it frees!

Amidst this vibrant, whimsy parade,
Life's a carnival, sweetly displayed.
With every step, we dance in flight,
To the cascade of joy, to the tropic light!

Winds that Cradle

Winds that cradle with a gentle tease,
Whispering secrets through bustling trees.
A dog in shade grins, tongue all a-loll,
Chasing swirling leaves, he has a ball!

Gusts of laughter flit by our ears,
As clouds trip over their fluffy fears.
A kite that's caught in playtime's snare,
Soars up and away, without a care.

The breeze lifts hats from folks that walk,
Playful pranks that the windy winds talk.
Giggles abound as waves kiss the shore,
This lighthearted symphony, who could ask for more?

So let's join the dance, come take my hand,
Let's bounce to the rhythm of this grand band.
With winds that cradle, we shall embrace,
This funny, fun-filled, timeless space!

A Symphony of Yellow Delights

In a jungle of laughter, quite a sight,
Fruity fellows dance in pure delight.
Yellow coats twirling, oh what a show,
Swinging to tunes of a sunny glow.

Chatter of monkeys, singing in trees,
Joyful sounds carried by a warm breeze.
Swinging through vines, what a merry spree,
A party of fruit, just you and me.

Mischief in motion, they bounce and sway,
Tickling the leaves, come join the fray.
A giggly parade, they leap with ease,
What a delight, this fruity tease!

With each playful wiggle, a chuckle we share,
Their silly shenanigans fill the air.
Oh, the joy as they jive and spin,
In this symphony of yellow, let the fun begin!

Fruity Fragrance in the Air

Whispers of sweetness float all around,
Golden delights on the ground abound.
A whiff of mischief, what could it be?
A fruity fragrance, wild and free.

Chasing the giggles, up in the trees,
Playful monkeys tease in the warm breeze.
Splashes of laughter, the sun shines down,
Twirling around in their yellow crown.

With every nibble, a silly cheer,
Frolicking friends who have nothing to fear.
Fruity adventures, oh what a ride,
Laughter erupts, we swing side by side.

A bouquet of antics, so light and bright,
Fruity fragrance dancing, pure delight.
In this merry realm, we shall stay,
Where joy and humor lead the way!

Shadows of a Sunny Delight

Beneath the canopy, shadows sway,
In a fruity world, we laugh and play.
Whimsical whispers, a silken tease,
With every shuffle, we move with ease.

Silly and bright, the shadows prance,
As wiggly critters join in the dance.
Giggles echo as they twirl with flair,
Creating laughter that fills the air.

Under the sun, in this joyous haze,
The shadows of smiles brighten our days.
A playful pop, a slide and a leap,
This sunny delight, we'll forever keep.

So let's swing and twirl, let laughter rise,
In the sweet shadows under sunny skies.
With each step taken, a grin we find,
In this fruity realm, we're one of a kind!

Lush Laughter Under the Sky

Under the sky, where the laughter flows,
Fragrant delights in a cheerful pose.
Twists and turns, such a merry spree,
Bubbly giggles dance, wild and free.

With playful pranks and silly tricks,
Bouncing along like a bag of bricks.
Colorful smiles with a splash of zest,
In the garden of joy, we're truly blessed.

Every chuckle rolls like the tide,
Sprightly friends rush in, no need to hide.
Wiggly and jiggly, they form a crew,
In this lush laughter, we'll start anew.

So gather around, let the fun ignite,
In a world of wonder, oh what a sight!
With joy in our hearts and humor so spry,
We'll dance forever, just you and I!

Dancing in the Canopy

With leafy floors beneath my feet,
I twirl and spin with joy, oh sweet.
The critters laugh, they join the play,
In the green haven, we sway all day.

A monkey swings and gives a cheer,
He throws a fruit, no need to fear.
It lands right near, it's quite the score,
As laughter echoes, we shout for more.

Squirrels join in, they flip and flop,
With every bounce, they never stop.
The sun peeks through, a golden ray,
While we all dance, hip-hip-hooray!

We shake our tails, we hug the trees,
In this wild world, we feel the breeze.
With each funny move, we feel so free,
In our playful jungle jamboree.

Sweetness in the Air

In the air, a scent so bright,
Like candy dreams in the morning light.
Critters clamor, they come to see,
What's that sweetness? Oh, let it be!

A parrot squawks, he starts to croon,
While beetles dance to a bopping tune.
The flowers blush, they join the fun,
As laughter spreads, we're all as one.

Fragrant whispers float all around,
With every chuckle, joy is found.
The buzz of laughter filled the air,
While silly antics banished despair.

Under the trees, we share a grin,
With friendly pokes and dips, we spin.
In the cloud of sweetness, we'll play and sing,
With every giggle, our hearts take wing.

Golden Flavors of the Dawn

Morning breaks with golden gleam,
In the jungle, life's a dream.
The sun spills joy in every ray,
And funny friends come out to play.

A hedgehog winked, he wore a hat,
He twirled around, how about that?
With flavors bright as morning dew,
It's playful joy, just us and you.

A skittering bug, a wobbly dance,
In the golden light, we take a chance.
We giggle loud, a chorus free,
As the breeze whispers secrets, just for we.

Each moment bursts with silly flair,
As laughter skips through the balmy air.
With every chuckle, life's a feast,
In the morning glow, joy never ceased.

Fragrant Sways

In the breeze, the flowers sway,
They giggle softly, come what may.
With scents that tickle every nose,
Their fragrant charm just overflows.

A chameleon blends with flair,
His colors shift, he doesn't care.
He swings his tail, gives a big wave,
With every move, he starts to rave.

The vines entwined, like laughter's sound,
As critters prance upon the ground.
We chuckle, roll, and spin around,
In the fragrant fun that's truly found.

A breezy tickle in the air,
With every giggle, we declare:
In this party made of glee,
Life's vibrant colors set us free.

The Golden Radiance of Life

In a grove where giggles grow,
Sunny fruit with a cheerful glow.
Slipping on peels, what a surprise!
Laughter echoes, reaching the skies.

Monkeys dance in wild delight,
Chasing tales through morning light.
In the shade, a joke is spun,
Life's a laugh, oh what fun!

With each bite, a chuckle bursts,
Sweetness quenches our funny thirsts.
We all roll in fruit-laden glee,
Nature's pranksters, wild and free.

So grab a snack, let joy ignite,
Life's a circus, a pure delight.
With smiles wide and spirits bright,
Savor the golden, laugh with might.

Caffeine of Paradise

Juicy gems like mugs of cheer,
Sip and smile, it's almost here.
Eager tongues, they slip and slide,
Sipping sunshine, let fun abide.

A prankster fruit on every plate,
Get ready now, there is no weight.
Playful bites, caffeinated fun,
Every morsel a silly run.

Munching leafy cosmic dreams,
In every laugh, a million beams.
Jesters of the orchard, bright and wild,
Fruitful giggles, chaos compiled.

Dive into joy, let sweetness flow,
Laughter's the drink we all know.
Euphoria bursts with every taste,
Paradise found, there's no time to waste.

Whirls of Painted Sunbeams

In a world of swirls and spins,
A fruity dance where laughter wins.
Colors whirl in a playful breeze,
Ticklish tastes that aim to please.

Squishy smiles on every face,
Fruity pranks, a zany race.
Slip and slide on sunny dreams,
Laughter erupts in joyful beams.

With every bite, a giggle forms,
Bouncing bright like cartoon storms.
Turquoise skies and lemony cheer,
Life's a jest, let's make it clear!

Round and round, the fun won't stop,
Fruity giggles make us hop.
In this whirl, we find our song,
With painted sunbeams, we belong.

Palettes of Flavor

Splashing colors of fruity cheer,
Each bite a canvas, taste sincere.
Artful munching, funny and bright,
Laughter swings into the night.

Every slice a vibrant jest,
Like a painter, we feel so blessed.
Whimsical bites delight our day,
Art of flavors, come out and play.

With squishy sketches on our plates,
Tasting joy, oh how it creates!
A palette full of sunny jest,
Life's sweet flavor is truly the best.

Merriment in every crunch,
Fruity magic packs a punch.
Let's paint the world with laughter's hue,
In this canvas, I find you.

The Joy Below the Canopy

Under leaves so wide and green,
Silly monkeys dance unseen.
They juggle fruit with playful flair,
The laughter floats upon the air.

With every slip and every slide,
A joyful cheer they cannot hide.
The sun peeks through, so bright and bold,
These tales of fun never get old.

A parrot squawks with pure delight,
Joining in the merry flight.
As fruits take flight from bumper boughs,
We laugh along, we share the vows.

In this playground of delight,
Life's a comedy in sunlight.
With every giggle, every tease,
We're swept away by nature's breeze.

Serendipity in the Sunshine

A gecko wearing shades of green,
Spots a snack, unseen, unseen.
Giggling softly, he does leap,
While all around, the critters peep.

A twisty vine now starts to sway,
As squirrels join the wild ballet.
They chatter tales of sweet surprise,
Beneath the bright, blue, cloudless skies.

A splash of color, funny noise,
The rustling leaves, the dancing joys.
With every bounce and every cheer,
You'd think the fruits would shed a tear!

So come away and take a chance,
Join in their playful, silly dance.
For nature's bounties brought with glee,
Are filled with secrets and jubilee.

Laughter Among the Yield

Among the branches, giggles rise,
As fruits dangle like curious spies.
A clumsy bear trips on a root,
His face in dirt, oh what a hoot!

The babbling brook laughs right along,
Echoing nature's cheerful song.
With each splash and joyful sound,
The whole world seems to spin around.

A salamander in a hat,
Takes on a dance, imagine that!
He twirls and spins with such a flair,
Who knew a critter could compare?

So gather 'round this playful yield,
Where joy and laughter are revealed.
With every twist and silly jest,
This nature's party is the best!

Nature's Flavored Wishes

In gardens lush, where colors blend,
The silly breezes twist and bend.
Wishes float like fluffy clouds,
Poking fun at all the crowds.

With every wink from sunlight's rays,
Critters gather for their plays.
A chubby rabbit hops around,
Stomping softly on the ground.

And oh, the fruits come out to laugh,
A zesty humor, quite the craft!
Their juicy giggles fill the air,
As nature shares its playful flair.

Among the vines, the fun is rife,
Beneath the trees, a merry life.
So let's embrace this comic scene,
Where laughter reigns, and hearts are keen.

Solstice Ripples

In the sun, we start to sway,
With a peel that brightens the day,
Laughter floats on a gentle gust,
In fruity joy, we place our trust.

Tropic tunes in the air grow loud,
Chasing shadows, we dance, so proud,
With every slip, a giggle's born,
Holding tight, but soon we're torn.

Bouncing bright like a summer's dream,
We leap and twirl, each twist a beam,
Nonsensical, our hearts unite,
In this playground of pure delight.

A splash of fun on a lazy tee,
With each burst, we roar, we flee,
In the warmth where we all just tease,
As we float on this silly breeze.

Radiant Horizons

Underneath the sunny skies,
We wear our smiles, oh so spry,
Chasing clouds with a silly plan,
Each giggle like a fruit-filled can.

A stroll through fields of buttercream,
Where every laugh is a honeyed dream,
In a world twirling like our hats,
We dance along with the furry cats.

Golden rays, our joyful hues,
Peels and laughter, we can't refuse,
In every moment, we take a chance,
Painting life with a goofy dance.

So let the echoes of joy resound,
In this gleeful playground found,
We'll skip and roll till the daylight fades,
A feast of fun in the sun's cascades.

A Symphony of Yellow

A cheerful tune in the summer air,
With smiles, we strut without a care,
Yellow giggles, a riotous show,
In this melody, we let it flow.

Each note slips like a playful wink,
With every twist, we start to think,
What if we seasoned our laughter well,
With sprinkles of joy that we can sell?

In a garden where silliness reigns,
We pluck delight like golden grains,
A chorus laugh, like candy bars,
As we bounce beneath the dance of stars.

Our symphony, a playful dread,
In every slip, a giggle spread,
With whimsy wrapped around our toes,
In a colorful world where happiness grows.

Chill of the Fields

In shady glades where the breezes tease,
We roll and tumble with so much ease,
In ridiculous poses, we strike a stance,
Each moment a chance for a silly dance.

A sweet surprise in the air around,
As laughter ripples through the ground,
With each echo, our spirits rise,
In fields of joy beneath the skies.

Drifting whims with a playful cheer,
Our antics, bright like the summer sphere,
Each falling leaf, a playful jest,
In nature's arms, we find our rest.

So let's embrace this jovial ride,
In a world where we all confide,
With warmth and laughter, the heart it yields,
In a silly charm, our joy reveals.

www.ingramcontent.com/pod-product-compliance
Lightning Source LLC
Chambersburg PA
CBHW060113230426
43661CB00003B/172